I0785746

Presentation.

Dear Readers:

I invite you to accompany me on this long journey, a journey that I will travel with those who do not want to be protagonists, the Syrian migrants, the sordid stories that develop and transcend to the side of an open road the passage by human traffickers, travelers with little baggage and no definite destination, except for the illusion of establishing itself in an uncertain country, and there a hypothetical new home; or by the icy and unknown Arctic mountains, a new route, more economical as well as longer, and ravaged by the mafias of migrant tracts; already in the dark bilge, or clinging to the wood of a rickety and insecure boat; or on board the fragility of a little wood boat, the fate of a tomb of more than one who manages to embark on it.

You go to know if in the border fences of a frizzy barbed wire, clinging, surviving the cruelty of border guards; or astride a white bicycle, painted thus by the snow, a singular means of transport abandoned then anywhere, fulfilled its purpose; It will be to walk, like a shadow to the helplessness of the frontier lines, or on the cold rails of a train from which they see their last wagon depart with the lost hope of occupying a seat in it, or to cling to any part of that swift traveler which is leaving, without even saying goodbye. It is a painful reality.

Tormented by the situations that have forced them to take the undesirable decision to make to the endless paths that remain to be traveled, to go back by any of the uncertain and dangerous routes, three, four, or any number of them, furrows open to shorten the unknown distances to which they add the immense risks in their attempt to reach its objective. It is to travel great extensions accompanied by the inclement sun, or by the darkness of darkness between roads and shortcuts, until reaching the rivelous coasts, some of them, of the Mediterranean to continue their incessant adventure by the dangerous waters of those seas after the search for European borders; or by land, privileging the reach of those countries that will provide, in saying, greater sum of benefits and quality of life.

Or reach them through the icy heights of the Arctic until they reach what they imagine is hiding behind their heights, which will be nothing more than the hope of crystallizing the longed for dream of establishing themselves in the country that grants them legal refugee reception, and the attempt will not be worth it either; Is to transit, to the support of illegality after his goal, all given to fate as the last refuge, less to back down in their attempt, Is to leave the walls of their houses, back in their village, to go in search of what is desired, what is their objective; Is to give way to the encounter with his utopia, with the alchemy of his dreams, or with his decisive determination to leave behind the horrors of war; Is a very high cost that led to statistics is very likely not reach their destination, however, is to suppose that the despair that embarrasses them will beyond thinking of a failure.

They will also carry in the intricacies of their mind the faces of those who caused their misery translated into a journey in its known starting point, but before an uncertain destiny, perhaps without return, of luck, say, application of the messages of their sacred books submitted to their interpretation, that not of the truth, or the cruelty of their truth, of those who did not establish social coexistence as a principle of life, or of the fellow beings who, imprisoned by their human miseries, have forced to make that decision, which is their fault, but those who in those confrontations for political or economic power, or a religion of which their preachers know, but do not share their interpretation.

All this, and how many more reasons they did not hasten to the emptiness of the unknown, to embark on that embarrassing route, dangerous challenge, in search of a destiny in whose origins, Syria destroyed by the war, was forced to undertake, all this, and how much more will not converge in the minds of these human beings when, with the dawn awakening, or at any hour of the day or night, harassed by the anguish, they gather in the modest baggage, if for that the road will claim him, that it will not be much that he takes and also to satisfy what the need will demand, and to think it or not to carry it, it will be a dilemma not possible, or difficult, to resolve when to make those roads urged by Insecurity of the war, internal conflicts or tensions of the same tenor, and the irreverent interpretation of the sacred book of his God, who harassed him become threatening fundamentalisms, gloomy sum of uncontrolled barbarism

What did not happen to the mind to those who ventured through the unfathomable paths of horror, the way of the bewilderment, the longing to reach the dream that crunches in the interiorities of his being, is to say a goodbye that fights to leave his throat, or to express a later one in which he himself hesitates to believe that that undeniable desire is fulfilled. It will be feeling strange, rare, inside of yourself.

Let us go, then, by the unfathomable paths of the unknown for those unlucky traveler's strangers of their land by the cruelty of a war.

Humberto Silva Cubillán.

Chapter I. Some considerations, at the beginning of the long way to go.

A multitude of human beings from that country that we encounter, in our imagination, and collecting information from the first pages of newspapers with the largest circulation worldwide, or television, which in real time transports us to the scenarios of the war that there, in Syria, develops; or the portals that have emerged and configured a new way of disseminating news, which abound in proportion to the development of technology and information; of non-governmental organizations (the officials in the programs of their duties), grouped together to give protection to those who flee from that country, or others, but always looking for the unknown destination, in the case that interests them, Europe; to accompany them on the routes drawn for their escape from the terrifying scene whose events they want to keep their distance, convulsed country left behind, pursuing what they would consider qualifying them for the recognition of refugee status, or other forms of protection in the countries of a hypothetical final destination, until and according to the definitions that in that sense are indicated by UNHCR and the legal instrument by which that organization of the UN is governed, consider them as.

Leaving behind his country is sad, in any circumstance, but more infamous even when the game is shaken by the situations that are vented in its streets, the capital, or in any city regardless of its demographic density or surface, Damascus ,

Deraa, Aleppo, a place of terrorist penetration, with all its humanitarian corridor that very few escape, desperate families who venture to leave behind their longing for their homeland, the daily life with their family so close , their evoked desires, harassed by an incomprehensible war, maze of conflicts for the most varied reasons, inexplicable more existent, there religious, fundamentalism that terrifies, Islam and Christianity of long tradition their confrontations, secular confrontations, even during In the last years, almost half a century, most of its Sunni Muslim population whose control is exercised by a fam Ilia of Alawites, teachings that derive of the chiismos since the century IX, evolution that follows from certain characteristics of the Christianity and of questionable preislámics cults; aand to those that exist since the intervention of Iraq, or well-known Iraq war, a coalition led by the USA, of which was left a bitter legacy: the confrontation between the West and followers of Saddam Hussein what became in a war between Sunnis and Shiites, and from there the presence of the ineffable and perverse Islamic State at the head of the Sunni contingents, and with the Shiites the Kurdish rebels, marked Syrian ethnic minority, who control some cities to the northwest of the tormented country.

These are the scenarios in which an unspeakable war unfolds, and the indescribable exodus of migrants in them, in their cities, on their borders with the Iraqi border areas that, although being a very important part and of supposed independence for the prevailing conflict, opposition of the Kurds to both President Al Assad and the Islamic State, has motivated the establishment of its own State on the borders between Syria and Iraq, or the undeniable presence of economic and political interests that roam the platforms of the important oil fields that try to control those groups and the countries involved; this is nothing more than what those who are part of the war face, civilians, potential refugees in the end, accuse the sequence of so many factors that lead to an impressive criminal violence in the theater of conflict.

Leaving behind his country is sad, in any circumstance, but more infamous even when the game is shaken by the situations that are vented in its streets, the capital, or in any city regardless of its demographic density or surface, Damascus , Deraa, Aleppo, a place of terrorist penetration, with all its humanitarian corridor that very few escape, desperate families who venture to leave behind their longing for their homeland, the daily life with their family so close , their evoked desires, harassed by an incomprehensible war, maze of conflicts for the most varied reasons, inexplicable more existent, there religious, fundamentalism that terrifies, Islam and Christianity of long tradition their confrontations, secular confrontations, even during In the last years, almost half a century, most of its Sunni Muslim population whose control is exercised by a family of Alawites, teachings that derive of the chiismos since the century IX.

Evolution that follows from certain characteristics of the Christianity and of questionable preislámicos cults; And those that exist since the intervention of Iraq, or well-known Iraq War, a coalition led by the USA, which left a bitter legacy: the confrontation between the West and Saddam Hussein's followers which resulted in a war between Sunnis And Shiites, and from there the presence of the ineffable and perverse Islamic State at the head of the Sunni contingents, and with the Shiites the Kurdish rebels, marked Syrian ethnic minority, who control some cities to the northwest of the tormented country.

Chapter II. Origin of the civil war in Syria.

Taking a stage as a reference to place ourselves in the context of the reality of current events, can be when the fires in the deserts were lit from the Arab Spring, a statement not always shared by analysts and scholars of war, with the destabilization of that country, Syria, which developed intensely at the beginning of the year 2011 with the effervescence of protests against the government which, in principle, did not obtain the results that the demonstrators expected, deducing the government that what was happening with the violent movements that waved to Egypt, Tunisia or Libya, would not happen there, seeing the results for that moment obtained, clearly, satisfactory.

With the participation of the activists through social networks, coordinated via the Internet, from March of that year an unexpected operation took place, for the government, a reversal reversing the situation: the youth protests became much stronger, especially in the main cities of the country, especially in Deraa, where the conflict was generated, in its beginnings; the clashes became more cruel, more and more, thousands of people according to their slogans came to the streets of that city bearing different emblems of the movement, to protest against the government, peaceful protest that ended up becoming an uprising that ended with the Fire of the Palace of Justice, the headquarters of the ruling Baath party and the building of the Syriatel telephone company.

The public force, using weapons, was not expected with one dead and several injured, hundreds of detainees among the demonstrators as a result of government repression that increased in the following days increasing the number of deaths, injuries and arrests, which inflamed more the moods between both positions in conflict seeing the government in the necessity to take to the street the army before the overflow of the units of the police forces on the part of the opponents, to try to quell the popular insurrection, something happening Unexpectedly: several military men in total disagreement with the brutal repression of the regime were insubordinate and, following that insubordination, would create the Free Syrian Army, also known as the Free Officers Movement, with the supposed objective of protecting the civilian population from the repression of the regime by means of the use of the arms, insurrects that stimulated by that support begins they were armed and assaulted police stations and police stations.

The establishment of the Syrian National Council, following the organization of the Free Syrian Army, whose foundations would be those of a body charged with representing the Syrian opposition politically and allowing the different rebel factions to be represented before the international community, gave rise to organizational visions of the libertarian movement, which in this way would undertake the search for the objectives proposed from its origins, but now under the leadership of men leaving the barracks, with military training and knowledge of the principles that governed war, tactics and strategies, as well as the distribution of their operational readiness, knowledge and conditions of the Armed Forces facilities, hence their progress towards the northern provinces in order to secure control of the border with Turkey would be an objective, movement which would allow them to be able to make arms, vehicles, supplies of logistic and medical supplies, and thus be able to deal with the government forces in other conditions, as a fact that, from these events, the civil war in Syria begins to develop.

Of the geopolitical importance of the region raised in flames from the events of Tunisia, the United States and its European allies saw the Arab Spring as a great economic opportunity, no wonder since that ingredient, oil, is still of interest in the equation of any conflict and has always been, even where they are appetizing deposits, as is the case, from which they deduced that with the advent of hypothetical democracy these countries would be allowed to open new markets and, In addition, to obtain new allies with which to strengthen its position in a complicated zone but of great strategic importance, therefore they focused their efforts in supporting the rebels, in the majority of the countries in conflict, or with visions of it to happen, support which was primarily political, military also in mind that in order to stay in force before its pretensions groups seeking to overthrow governments they would need weapons and logistics in all their expressions: supplies, financing, logistics and a large part of military advisers, which could precipitate victory and, hence, the assumption of power by part of the insurgents.

To all these, the results were not going to give according to their expectations (that of the North Americans, Russians and allies, par excellence, economic ends, also those of Qatar) since the insurrection phenomenon in each country had different shades, in Libya, for example, the root of the uprising was, at any event, the inspiration born in the sands of Tunisia, extracted from the results of the aforementioned Arab Spring: social conflict and the presence of a tyranny that plunged its people In general, but the result was a situation where the various tribes fought for power, with the characteristics of that reality: the social, political and economic functioning characterized by having a government that had little control over vast regions of its territory, it did not provide basic services, proliferation of corruption and of criminality, as well as a marked economic degradation.

Four years after the beginning of the Libyan uprising, the armed uprising against the Gaddafi dictatorship, since February 17, 2010, ignited the fires of the

Maghreb, north of the African continent, in a geopolitical conception of this region whose coasts are in the Mediterranean Sea to the North, the Atlantic Ocean to the West and the Sahara Desert to the south, consisting of Mauritania, Morocco, Algeria, Libya, Tunisia and Western Sahara , after long contradictions and clashes, in April 1976 Mauritania and Morocco signed an agreement in Rabat that divided Western Sahara, two thirds further north for Morocco and the remaining third for Mauritania, facing the dictatorships of the region; the insurrection of the Libyan people who were suffering the rigors of Gaddafi's dictatorship triggered eight months of a violent civil war that ended the fall of the regime embodied in the capture and death of the dictator.

Paradoxically, there remained signs of the atmosphere of the widespread euphoria that was installed, ephemerally, after the so called Arab Spring, a word that for this community has been no more than a painful irony since the prosperity augured was no more than a mere fantasy and the transition to a democratic system was soon to be put to fruition in the absence of strong institutions that would take over the process and make themselves trusted by the Libyan people.

Today, according to the national consensus, little has been demonstrated that it was something like a chimera and, not in vain in the country there are two rival parliaments that operate simultaneously, one in Tripoli, and one more than a thousand kilometers to the east, In Tobruk, If the United States is involved, providing the rebels with modern weapons, ammunition and medical supplies, in addition to providing money and sending military experts to advise and train their troops, in the face of Russia's support for Bashar al-Assad , and the fear of turning Syria into a new Iraq; gave with the fret to a possibility of American invasion to that country, at that time.

In order to avoid a confrontation and support to the elements in conflict, each one of the powers in its own way and with ends found: the Syrian government, Russia and the USA, to those opposed to that dictatorship rebel groups , a situation that has varied ostensibly when Russia, USA and France are going to form a broad coalition, which has given a turn to the criteria before, after two events that forced such determination: bloody attacks in Paris and the explosion of the Russian A321 aircraft, which despite the Egyptian authorities disagree with the results of the Russian investigation, that it was the product of an attack by the Isis, who had already attributed it; has motivated to face the situation joining the efforts, to which have been added other countries.

The Muslim Brotherhood in Egypt, based on Islamic radicalism, although in its beginnings supported in a biased way the coup d'état of July 2013 with which the military regained power over the country, under the guise of reinstating democracy the western powers terrified by the way the government of the Muslim Brotherhood took changed their attitude. In the case of Syria, the country that has been the main exporter of migrants, US and European support for the rebels, was, and still is, with the fatal results, very evident and based on a truth: already traditional rejection of dictatorships to democracies and vice versa, hence strategically a change of government in Syria, greatly improve the important situation of the US and its allies in the Middle East and at the same time would weaken that of its main rival: Russia. Those were their calculations, apparently, and the face of the events of the year 2015, was not so true, the implementation of that strategy, we intuit, and then before the terrorist acts in Paris, and the subject of the Russian aircraft, changed the position from both powers and allowed to speak of a broad coalition against the Islamic State.

Syrian conflict, as well as government support, Hezbollah, which in alliance with Lebanon and Syria itself, have remained in open confrontation against Israel, and on this front its recharge to the Syrian rebels, supported by the Americans, which has been his argument to intervene in the conflict with visible results in favor of the government, when a capture of some of the localities that was previously in the hands of the rebels, has allowed the opening of the roads that lead to the port of Tortous, In the Mediterranean, where the Russian base is and from there the access to the resources that that country provides to the Syrian government.

Unwilling attendants, uninvited, will join in the conflict in that country, Syria, when fundamentalist, radical, Islamist groups have faced the evils of confrontation between groups, government, rebels and Hezbollah (ISIS), whose roots have been in Iraq since 2006, in order to confront the Americans at that time, becoming foreign fighters, ultra conservative Sunnis from Iraqi Kurdistan and Al Qaeda ally, which is going to lose, that is to say, after the results of their confrontation in Iraq, unsuccessful, however in 2010, with the arrival of Abu Bakr al-Baghdadi, new and charismatic leader, the presence of this group takes other paths.

It will restart its terrorist crusade in Iraq and at the same time would extend to the north of Syria, before the inconsistency of the Syrian ruler, Assad, to maintain in the power, and in 2013 proceeds of the "Islamic State of Iraq and the Levant," attacking both government troops and rebels alike, extending its power until it gained control of Iraq and Syria, when, a year later, after the capture of the North of Iraq, its leader would proclaim itself as Caliph of that new terrorist state, instituting its version of the Sharia, Islamic Law, severely punishing to those who violate it, chasing to the religious minorities, executing prisoners and spreading by social networks its frightening actions.

.

And now, the Islamic State, caliphate, a state form led by a political and religious leader in accordance with Islamic law, controls a territory between Syria and Iraq and which seeks to receive full support from the Muslim world, an organization that is one of the greater threats to the security, not only of Syria but of the whole world for the cruelty of its actions, there: mass murders, kidnappings of religious minorities and beheadings spread on social networks, wave of fear and hatred throughout the world, increased by the events of Paris and the Russian plane, which shocked society; actors who as a whole have been confabulated to cause the social, political and economic instability of the planet.

The presence of these actors, members of the Islamic State, started in 2002, when Abu Musab al-Zarqawi, of Jordanian origin, at the head of the radical group Tawhid wa al-Jihad, swears after the invasion of the United States to Iraq, loyalty to Osama bin Laden, founds al Qaeda in Iraq, a group that became the greatest force raised in arms during the years of the American occupation, a movement that after Zarqawi's death in 2006, al Qaeda created an alternative organization called the Islamic State of Iraq (ISI), a group that will not withstand the onslaught of US forces, in addition to the Sahwa council, led by Sunni tribes who were not In agreement with the cruelty of the newly nominated ISI, emerging from there a new leader, in 2010, Abu Bakr al-Baghdadi, who is going to readjust the organization and the subsequent attacks against the Syrian president; It merges the militias in Iraq and Syria and denominates them Islamic State of Iraq and the Levant.

The leaders of the Nusra front, formed by Sunni Islamist mujahideen, whose aim was to overthrow the Assad government to create an Islamic state under the Sharia, moral code and religious law of Islam, and establish a Caliphate, try to recruit all Syrians to that they take part in the war against the government with which they had fought against the Assad, but they rejected the decision being only followed by Abu Bakr, who agreed with the establishment of a jihad, religious decree of war based on the Koran, appeal which extends from the law of God.

In December 2013 ISIS took up arms in Iraq and took advantage of the deep political divide between the Shi'a-oriented government, a Muslim sect which claims that only Ali and his descendants are the only legitimate caliphs, and the Sunni minority, mainstream of Islam, aided by the tribal leaders, managed to control the city of Falluja, some 69 km west of Baghdad, on the banks of the Euphrates, known as the "City of Mosques", because there are more than two hundred in the city, and the villages of the surroundings; but the real blow came in june of that year when they seized control of Mosul, the second city of the country, and continued their advance toward the capital, Baghdad. In mid-July they had consolidated their control over dozens of cities and towns, from which ISIS declared the creation of the caliphate and changed its name to that of Islamic State.

Chapter III. The intensification of the conflict.

The civil war in Syria, which seems to have no solution, or at least omens to get out of the complicated situation, on the contrary tends to worsen more and more before the advance of the Islamic State which has led to the flight of thousands of people of that country, emigrants who flee to Europe due to aggravated civil conflict; already has more than five years, crisis that has originated that mobilization that tries to escape the conflict and the advance of the terrorist group in that country, massive exodus that not only refers to those that will have reached the objective of its daring, but those who have left their life on the road, those numbers and those that will increase substantially making statistics increasingly difficult, as well as the unwillingness of the European countries of destination, or reception, to be given acceptance.

The growth of the Syrian population, in proportion to those who have left their places of birth, has also complicated the picture as this has a direct impact on infrastructures affected by the effects of the conflict and the lack of technical, economic and of staff to tackle the solution of problems, and the economy is in an extreme situation, according to the UN, which estimates to date, which varies according to the daily circumstance, that 12.2 million people need help within of Syria, of which 7.6 million are displaced, a classification defined by UNHCR, and those that remain in that country will be the families, not necessarily, who have not been able to take the road of those who would be inscribed in the classification of refugees .

Also clarified its definition, armed conflict that has already been located in its sixth year and these are the figures that the investigations of the organisms as well as its consequences have been decisive for a significant part of the population to make their decisions, people who have been forced to flee to neighboring countries, and violence continues to grow in northern Syria and Its western border, hence the painful results: 220,000 dead, 11 million displaced, 3.9 million refugees and 12.2 million people who depend on humanitarian aid to survive and have not been possible to achieve peace, as it will hardly be before these circumstances, origins that in the Arab Spring therefore rebelled against dictatorial governments, flares that traveled the deserts of the Middle East in which it prevailed: corruption, poverty, violation of human rights, underlining in these factors, social inequality.

Phenomena embedded in the administration and public policies that have not or have not willingly disposed of the will, and if impunity, to sanction, or at least to neutralize, and to end the injustice and inequality that were the origins of this conflict and which have not ceased to be present until today, along with the different parties involved increase their warlike actions with materials and equipment, financial and logistical support from organizations in the Islamic world, which they provide, fight and end with a civilian population that lives in fear and tries to survive, a painful equation of which children who at a young age have grown up under the noise of weapons of war, away from classrooms, victims of rape, forced to enlist in their organizations, women who cannot give birth in hospitals because hospital facilities, violating the articulation of the Geneva Conventions of 1949 and its 2 Additional Protocols of 1977, have been attacked, destroyed or in any case because medical or paramedical personnel have been killed.

An alarming situation that has become part of the lives of all those who, inevitably, approach the screens of televisions, even in real time, when they happen those events in the world, scenarios of war, conflicts of any kind, tensions and internal disturbances where they are not part of that situation, more if passive elements that suffer the consequences of a confrontation generally alien to its causes, that will be of others and their interests, of survival at the best, those of potential migrants, displaced or refugees a posteriori, if they survive in the daring adventure; but not the confrontation as a means for the resolution of their conflicts, which are seen faces transformed by the terror reflected in the photos that have been responsible for transmitting, even crudely, the international television networks that have developed to the In line with the demands and advances of information   and   communication   technology.

Presence of social networks, and of non-governmental organizations or international organizations that have made the calamities suffered by those in political, social or economic situations, decide to leave their countries becoming refugees, or displaced, according to the case and qualify for it, of which in important part we have been worth to approach to that reality that is in full development, and very far from the keyboard of our computer, diffusion of the news that revolves around this communicational phenomenon, even in direct, devices ranging from cable television and satellite, portals, drones, websites and radio stations, 24 hours a day, in several languages, giving a vision, according to critics, very parceled out of the world reality .

What they do under the optics of the same interpretation of the news, when it is dealt with, and being located in the western world they differ from a channel that emerged in the Arabic television media, Al Jazeera, the main news channel of that Arab world, from which opinions are given according to their criteria and also, parceled out to their interests, conflict scenarios, of which they live, like the western channels, and what they appreciate their news and scenes, the darker, be an important role that the Internet played in these revolutions, initiated by the so-called Arab Spring, divided opinions as to the positive or negative that this has been, at best, if these means have been of capital importance as technology of communications and information in the life of society today, at any level and country, not less their presence in those events their difference could have been marked in such revolutions developed in the hot sands of deserts, network that with their spontaneity and far from being capitalized on by anybody in particular, perhaps if some group that was characterized by that, exposed what the governments concealed.

The emigrants in the scene of the war.

To propose, alone or in the company of the family, to take to the turbulent waters of the sea, or to face the treachery of the treacherous sands of the deserts, or the cruelty of the cold of the Arctic, to shorten the way in search of the destiny of its the reality, painful reality that we are seeing in these times, the forced mobilization of so much population from the Middle East, Africa, the Western Balkans and South Asia, towards Europe, which has generated a complicated humanitarian situation in the that converges a varied human typology that is reflected in the increase of a growing and uncontrolled transit of beings, a posteriori in search of the qualification of refugees, already defined, and differentiated, by the UNHCR, from the concept of displaced ; asylum-seekers and Refugees, tend to be confused, the one requiring recognition of the status of "refugee" and whose application has not yet been evaluated in final form ; Economic emigrants, who distance themselves from the concept of "refugees" because he is the one who is induced to leave his country of origin for personal reasons, seeking new horizons and living standards, of the circumstances to try to be considered as beneficiary of the measures that are taken for the solution of their situation.

Chapter IV. Survival, particular objective.

According to the Convention relating to the Status of Refugees, adopted at Geneva on 28 July 1951 by the Plenipotentiary Conference on the Status of Refugees and Stateless Persons (United Nations) convened by the General Assembly in its resolution 429 of 14 December 1950, entered into force on 22 April 1954, in accordance with Article 43; Refugee is one who: "as a result of events occurring before 1 January 1951 and because of well-founded fears of being persecuted for reasons of race, religion, nationality, membership of a particular social group or political opinion, is outside the Country of its nationality and cannot or, because of such fears, does not wish to avail itself of the protection of that country; or who, lacking nationality and being, as a consequence of such events, outside the country where he had his habitual residence, cannot or, because of such fears, does not want to return to him. "

Unlike today's "refugee", properly identified as such, who fled by persecution, generalized violence or massive violation of human rights, and other migrants in vulnerable condition; In the face of the attacks in Paris, governments turned their attention to the group calling itself the Islamic State, extremists who claimed responsibility for the attacks, killing at least 127 people, a terrorist one Its power document that accredited to him like refugee that together they share the routes of irregular displacement towards countries of the European Union, in this case, what has aggravated the situation by the increasing arrival, by any means, and through the dangerous ones Cruises by the Mediterranean Sea; or the Arctic polar circle; Or southeastern Europe, people eager to find, even at the risk of their own lives, a place where they have legal, social and economic security, which in their countries of origin are denied them.

The dangerous uncertainty of the routes.

In the way of knowledge, we express it shallowly, of the reasons that motivate them, well-known of what drives them to leave behind their homes, is the dilemma of the routes and destiny of so many people who are often referred to as migrants , Being no more than many people, whole families, who risk their lives to escape the reality that is lived in their countries of origin, Syria in our case of follow-up, causing, or contributing to this the humanitarian crisis that is in full development in Europe.

To try to reach their goal, those who pretend to achieve it, even contempt of their own lives and those who accompany them in the adventure, there are several and risky routes to reach any destination, men, women and children who try to reach the old continent by the dangerous roads on foot, or by any means that favors them: seafarers, always the Mediterranean to cross, through Italy, Greece, or the Strait of Gibraltar, not easy to beat, is a little more distant to reach its intended way to Spain, through Ceuta or Melilla, fragile little wood boat by means, then wire fences in its boundaries, difficult to climb and to try, there the border guard to the hunt to avoid it; and bypassing the icy paths of the Arctic, from there to Russia and Serbia, access to follow and direct their steps towards Germany, precious destination to reach, or any of the countries of northern Europe, preferably, will be what is inscribed in their movements.

Syria, which has become the largest supplier of migrants, not very encouraging place, who are anxiously seeking some host country, preferably Europe, and there also want to privilege their demands in countries of their predilection, Germany, among them, conjunction of evils which seems to be embedded in that society that seeks to open itself to other horizons in the face of the calamities of war and its aftermath caused by the parties to the conflict: the government, rebels and other religious groups, countries linked by political and economic interests, among others factors that converge in the described scenario.

For example, the rebels have tortured and executed hundreds of soldiers, police and sympathizers of the regime, and government forces, also committed all atrocities against prisoners and civilians, torture, indiscriminate bombings, in violation of the IV Geneva Conventions of 1949 and the Second Additional Protocols of 1977, we also included in the International Treaties, the 1954 Hague Convention for the Protection of Cultural Property, violated upon seeing the ancient archaeological heritage destroyed, looted and sold to International collectors, or devastated by barbarism, enculturation and radical religious beliefs; in addition to the suffering derived from famines, epidemics, lack of medical services, lack of security, and from there: robberies, kidnappings, sexual assaults and rapes, all this, in short, conspires against peace that such a society demand.

Aborted to other countries, where they are even stigmatized, immigrants, not yet considered as refugees until they have been accepted as such by the host countries and society, where they can hardly arrive, and from there subjected to a follow-up that allows them to express an opinion about their behavior, but always stigmatized socially, disadvantaged by racial, religious, ethnic issues and given that they arrive there in such precarious economic conditions, health, work, education, culture; human condition that is not nested in the reasoning of the authorities that are invaded their countries by this avalanche, I end up little accepted by the NGOs, given that they are human beings; constitute an additional burden for these nations, and are therefore reluctant to receive them by the hypothetical recipient governments, to the detriment of their nationals who, with their labor, taxes, laws, contribute to their needs, and local, regional, and national governments, to pay them what they partially cancel with their contributions.

Immigrants have created a disconcerting migratory and humanitarian crisis in Europe, marked in the countries of origin by: wars, conflicts and internal tensions, religious differences, persecution, poverty, massive human rights violations and transnational criminal networks. Smuggling of migrants and trafficking in persons, for the purpose of exploitation, mainly women and children; creating with it a crisis in constant development whose incidence falls on some countries of the old continent, international regulation that was not structured in its original article to deal with the situations that today are presented, hence that great efforts are made to mitigate its consequences, In the host countries, when their situation is resolved, offering the victims a degree of international protection of assistance and, eventually, helping them to insert themselves in a new life.

Protection that can contribute to finding a general solution, but by increasing drastically the number of refugees in the last decades, as has been happening with this wave of arrivals by any means and trying to insert itself in the country that is most convenient to them; It has been emphasized that humanitarian work cannot substitute for the political action of the states that are suffering the consequences when it comes to solving what is evidently cracking the society in its context and affecting the economy of the countries subject to That contingency, of being of passage or welcome, of so many people, or avoid this bewildering situation that seems extreme.

The refugees, a reserve kept from this qualification until they are classified as such, Syrians, or in the clearest concept of them and to which we give special treatment in this work, those who aspire to be legally considered as such, regardless of the difficulties that they are aware of this, entails the undertaking of the long and dangerous crossing, by any of the defined routes, and milestones traced by the traffickers; are going to continue trying to cross the borders towards the European Union, and finish or not the war that in his country is developed, and in the best of cases that it ends, regardless of the reasons or causes that for it as well as who is credited with the success of the reasons that led to it.

The chances that the people who left their land and who, having reached their goal of crossing borders and arriving in Europe, hardly returned, either because of their establishment in the host country, security that was lacking there, the time it takes to recover the economy deteriorated by the effects of the war, social security levels, economic, legal, which they doubt , it is very likely to develop intransigence and reprisals between the parties that were in conflict ; the exodus will continue and, hardly, you will never know how long it will last.

The access routes to their requirements, place of destination, that of those who will be registered in the future in the classification of refugees, who have been called that way although not having arrived at their destination and obtained that classification, are the routes established by organizations that operate outside the law of trafficking in persons, reasons that could be found in the absence of regulations and control by the states, a little difficult to formulate given the circumstances in which they are and where civil wars do not give much space for it, except the corruption that generates, which would not be more than the letter printed in a paper whose articulation is not fulfilled, luck of utopia, then; It is these groups that set the costs, which vary due to the difficulties of each route, per person, or family if applicable, kilometers traveled, border crossing points, means to use and ineffable customs, whose managers will see in that process a way to obtain, supposedly, dividends by the concessions that grant to those who capitalize this informal traffic of people.

The Balkan route.

The Balkan route, an escape route to freedom, begins in Greece, it is from there that the migrants continue their journey, initiated in Syria, embarking towards Macedonia, then the crossing will be on foot through Serbia, Croatia and Slovenia, to the destination imagined that it could be Austria, Germany and the same Scandinavian countries, migratory route replaced by another one that took them from Turkey (where the main networks of smuggling of people operate, in cities as Istanbul, Izmir, Edirne and Ankara) to Algeria, because this country did not require a visa. This route, that of the Balkans, is considered the second route of migrants to Europe, the main one being that of the central Mediterranean, by Italy and Malta, most used by Syrian migrants to enter the old continent.

This route, although it is not the transit route for the largest number of migrants whose final destination is Europe, income that has been reduced due to the controls established by Turkey and Greece itself (Syrian migrants in a greater proportion, also its share of Afghans, Somalis and a progressive number from sub-Saharan Africa); Is perhaps the safest, in comparison with the Central Mediterranean, that being the one with the highest income of people, so is the one in its records that rests the record of the greatest number of people who could not reach their goal perishing in the attempt in the waters of the sea.

Lampedusa, a small Italian island, has acquired notoriety, not very grateful to the local authorities for this qualification, a product of the number of migrants who daily land on their coasts, also the highest rate of shipwrecks at sea due to the precariousness of the boats, excessive number of people on board and the prevailing weather conditions. A series of factors, of the most varied, will operate in the rates of transfer, or accompaniment, in the trip from an origin to a destiny previously contracted, is like, for example: the dangers to be overcome; the distances to be traveled; of whether it is by land or sea, as much as they can be mixed as well.

 The difficulty of crossing frontier posts, some more, others less vulnerable than others, as well as the leniency or demands of border guards, or access tariffs; agreements between countries of origin with Europe, or between those of common borders, such as the Schengen Agreement, which may vary from one side of the line to the other; are variables that operate at the time of negotiating the migrant with the trafficker. Here it imposes the rule and the interested party: the alternative to take or reject it, the adventure of making the journey, on its own carries more risks than usual, where reprisals may be another variable and the one that threatens the chances of success, although none of the options guarantees anything, trafficker is possibly the least risky, if perhaps the most expensive.

Overcoming the difficulties that will happen due to the factors and elements of the escalation of the conflict, which forces them to seek a forced departure from the country they are trying to flee, Syria, which since 2011 has been increasing cruelty and brutality of the authorities and organizations of any nature, but always criminal their actions to maintain the power, or to acquire it, according to the doctrine that guides them in their objectives; In order to escape this situation, thousands of people have moved to neighboring countries, such as Jordan, Lebanon, Turkey, Iraq and Kurdistan, transit territories in which they hardly want to remain given that the situation in them varies little in relation with which they leave behind, their country.

It begins the journey through the unpredictable to walk through the unknown, hard days on foot and, to arrive at the coasts, take to the sea where they await an uncertain destination, or die on the journey, is a long pilgrimage in which they can find In all their trajectory, the difficulties that must be solved by those who venture to escape from the city, or from the town where the start of their departure is located, to overflow the frontier boundaries of the starting country, to Turkey, a dividing line between the two countries, land and sea, which starts at the confluence of the triple border with Iraq and ends in the west, encountering the Mediterranean Sea, control of the Turkish border territory under NATO, which has turned that area into a high voltage strip.

Given the circumstances and events of 2012, due to Turkey's position in the area of tensions and internal disturbances, escalating the civil war in Syria, diplomatic relations between Turkey and that country were seen which led to Turkey's militarization of the border and it is from there that some enter Europe through Istanbul, Izmir, Edirne and Ankara, overcoming, if possible, the **trafficking** networks of persons operating in that Country of transit to final destination, Europe, route terrestrial most used by that permanent transhumance, however as an alternative most of them do it by sea taking the route to the Greek islands, risking their life in the waters of the Mediterranean, from Greece they continue, by land, to Macedonia, continue their long and desperate Serbia and from there until it reaches the border with Hungary, arriving at the entrance of the European space of free movement of people.

Macedonia and Serbia do not integrate the Schengen zone, space created in 1995 by the Agreement of Schengen to eliminate common borders between member countries and establish common border controls in those countries) and from Budapest try to travel by train to northern Europe, to reach the final destination of their adventure: Germany or the now the distances, risks, dangers arising from the threats of the Daesh, an insurgent, fundamentalist, jihadist, caliphate terrorist group, defined by its laws, settled in a vast territory of Iraq and Syria, are the main causes they incite the populations to risk their lives in interminable crossings.

Once on European soil and the desire to attain refugee status, their goal is to reach Germany, but that longing, or pretense, for their demand, entails severe sequelae for countries such as Serbia, Hungary or Austria, on the road to that expectation because it affects them by virtue of the fact that these governments must manage to attend to that number of people who, in an unexpected way if they want, they are altered their economies by the social and economic costs that this generate.

So that in Hungary the migrants who manage to get there will see the hours pass between hunger and discomfort, insecurity and extortion, which result from the conditions of such precariousness that they find, and on how to solve their the initial stage is how to overflow the boundaries separating them from Serbia, what they do, whether they can do it, through tunnels of the railways, or bypassing the metal fences and barbed wire that identify the border between the two countries, Serbia and Hungary, (about a meter and a half high, of wire, we would say, crowned with a spiral of barbed wire, is deployed along the 175 kilometers from the border with Serbia), waiting to be admitted to a "reception center", which is no more than a pretended attempt to give them better treatment and consideration, when what they find there is a camp without some areas of about 200 to 300 meters, a number of dozens of military tents under which there are beds for a number of people whose quantity has exceeded the capacity of accommodation and logistics, precarious conditions, without the most elementary standards sanitary and nutritional.

Vigilance is the responsibility of the police to impose the law, in their own way, to include there not even the population closest to the aforementioned "reception centers", that is: no one can get close to taking something to eat or remedy the most elemental of sanitary nature, if it were the case.

Austria has not stopped being affected, from there it has reinforced the control in its territory to prevent the traffic of people and to avoid misfortunes as it has been happening, sites of convergence that agree from the most varied ways other emigrants coming from Afghanistan, like also from Bangladesh, but those from Syria, children, elderly people or of any age, who are the only way to identify them is to place a bracelet with a number, nationality and date of arrival at the camp, which will have difficulty access to a ration of water, waiting to embark them on a train, to achieve a position always with difficulty if family groups is treated, heading to Budapest, transit papers as the only reference.

Although a good part of the migrants managed to reach Europe, crossing the Greek-Macedonian border with the Balkan route, more than 30,000 of them were waiting to cross, they were blocked at the greek border, and those who succeeded caught on the road, reaching a number of 65,343 people who irregularly attempted to cross the border and were detected by the border control agency of the European Union, being returned to the Greek islands through Turkey, after the signing of the Agreement.

The vicissitudes of the Arctic route.

29

The Arctic circle is the route increasingly used, when before it was reduced to a certain number of those who ventured through these glaciers, and it was a dozen Syrians who in the year 2014 used it to find a country to settle in fleeing from the civil war that ravaged, and ravages, their country, from there it has gone, progressively, increasing, following the roads that lead them from Russian territory to Norway, traditional country of reception of migrants, that is not member of the European Union, but it is part of the Schengen free transit area.

The crossing of the border crossing of Storskog (in this town many Syrians have stayed to live there, which shows that although they flee from war, it is not properly due to needs or hunger), near the city of Kirkenes, in the extreme north of the country, which has overwhelmed the authorities not prepared for this contingency, being forced to open mountain lodges, tents, until the rehabilitation of a hotel, which is in the process of adaptation to that type of visitor.

From Lebanon, from Syria, who aspire to make the journey through the Arctic, must obtain the visa granted by Russia, in their delegation in that country of origin of the trip, bought the ticket by plane to Moscow, there operate the travel agencies duly registered for this purpose, as is usual in any country, the journey continues by train to the north of the country, St. Petersburg, located in the north-west of the territory, on the Baltic coast, of great geopolitical and strategic importance for Russia, and whose cultural references bear the names with which they are often referred to as "The Venice of the North," "The Palmira of the North," and the "Cultural Capital of Russia," are some of the names with which usually refers to that city, the second Russian city in importance and population, unnecessary reference to the purposes of this population in pilgrimage of another nature, less cultural, therefore no interest will represent it.

And then continue to Murmansk, here was operating a business of the local Russian authorities that was concerned with travel, illegally traded and that the Norwegians put in control, that is where the use of the bicycle originates to get around the road of 20 kilometers separating Norway of Russia, in Storskog, border crossing between both countries with temperature not exceeding zero degrees, port city of Russia in the extreme northwest of the country, north coast of the peninsula of Kola, at the mouth of the Kola river in front of the sea Barents and near the Russian border with Norway and Finland, Russia's largest port, already in the Arctic circle itself.

Used by thousands of Syrian, Iraqi and Afghan migrants to cross the Russian-Norwegian border, nearly 200 kilometers of land border between the two countries, for that summer route, more cost-effective and risky than the more expensive Mediterranean, proportionately this since it supposes to play the life in the dangerous and turbulent waters of the sea; but are at risk because of the decision by the nordic authorities to deport those with a Russian visa, once migrants obtain a tourist or student visa once in Russian territory, so that they can legally travel by train to the region of Murmansk, border with Norway, and remain days or weeks in that country, which are the majority.

Norway has closed the Arctic border with Russia by the wave of Syrian migrants, a divide where thousands of them cross the Arctic Circle every day, bypassing the inclement temperature in terms of degrees below zero, and the snowfall that is huge as well as the partial reform of a law to expedite the expulsion of emigrants from Russia, and alert to the Syrians crossing the Russian border by bicycle.

Hungary has reinforced the border in the presence of them and threatens to use the Army, to prevent crossing the border line goes beyond the existence of some regulations that express it, more than this is the way that the Russian border guards have prevented access on foot, for the five kilometers that divide at that time both they allow it in cars, since the Norwegian authorities accuse people of trafficking in persons who help migrants to cross the border in their vehicles, thereby obliging the Syrians or any to do it on a bicycle, a business that has arisen at the helm of this imposed modality, generous in terms of foreign exchange, as well as some extra to teach them to pedal on the snow, basically the Arabs and Afghans, who in their life imagined having to learn to use that mode of transport and much less under those atmospheric conditions.

Failure to have access to the country on the other side of the line, Norway, forces them to stay for long periods, from the summer, and after the end of the strenuous crossing, in Russian border towns, which will be doing their business, there: hotels, apartments, houses, cafes, shops and local restaurants; the inhabitants of these communities will face a phenomenon that would not exist before: insecurity.

The Syrian refugees, in the equation of conflict temptation to extort migrants who must pay a minimum of 500 dollars to cross the border, has also surfaced there, something very widespread in any authority, who sees on that occasion to become an extra to remedy what the salary does not allow it, this being a mere assumption. The glacial winds also make their contribution to the difficulties of those who arrive in search of a way to cross the border, which before the refusal of the authorities to allow them to overcome the barrier, the way back is expedited, always on the rented bicycle or purchased, until the following day, and to cross the border, and to tread Norwegian territory, automatically apply for political asylum.

In recent weeks the "Arctic route" has lost some interest among the Syrians, who traveled with entire families, but not the same with the Afghans, who represent more than half of the total, and also now come immigrants from Asia and Africa, mostly young men. In any case, their plans are in danger, as the Norwegian Government Survival, sole objective would announce that it would immediately return to Russia all asylum seekers who had been legally resident in this country, whether by visa, residence permit or dual citizenship.

In addition, it would tighten the requirements for granting asylum and allow family reunification, and the only exception would be those with a Schengen visa, which is very difficult to find among the refugees who choose this marathon route. For its part Moscow claims that its border guards cannot force foreigners to show them their entry visas in Norway, since their stay in Russia is absolutely legal.

The Mediterranean route, through North Africa.

Along these routes, those who usually arrive to Greece from Turkey in boats of dubious quality and preparations for that voyage, otherwise dangerous given the turbulence of that sea, after a short sea crossing, since the dangers threaten the safety of the travel, continue through Macedonia and Serbia, final destination that is none other than Germany or another Syrian refugees, in the equation of conflict as a result of the prolongation of the Syrian conflict and the degradation of the situation in the bordering countries which led to more and more people joining the people of other origins who were headed towards the European Union, and with no possibility of returning to their native country, and the fear of closing the accesses, mechanisms of the most varied that are taking for the bordering countries, the European borders.

You have pressed them to break through any path, overcoming the costs and risks. well, this is one of them, which has been described the routes of refugees, this being the most used, as well as the most dangerous, which together with the operations of the European authorities against traffickers, has forced them to reorient those who flee their countries, driven by the same traffickers, to take other routes, formerly those of the Balkans, the most in demand.

The risks of crossing the Mediterranean, from Libya to Italy on inadequate ships, Survival, sole objective overloaded with passengers, to which is added the precarious conditions, lacking engines capable of mobilizing so many people, more than the capacity that would fit in their limited dimensions, without lifeguards, or at least those necessary for the proportion of people who embark; You have succeeded in the dead at sea, between Africa and Italy, completing a truly chilling number to mention.

Libya, via the Mediterranean Sea, without doubt the most dangerous, there converge those deprecated by wars and internal conflicts: those of Somalia, prey to a long, 26 years of cruel civil war; Those of Eritrea, with a third of the population in exile as a result of a Soviet style dictatorship, a reminder of the USSR's flourishing years in Africa; of South Sudan, where ethnic conflicts and the ineffable and persistent famines have been gathering since the 1960s; as of Nigeria and its caliph of Boko Haram, deployed in the north applies Sharia, code of strange justice, accepted by sectors of the population of the north, not admitted in the south, with a Syrian refugees, in the equation of conflict determinant proportion of christians, is considered an organization that manifestly supports terrorism against the civilian population and uses violent and coercive means in the pursuit of its political religious objectives, adhered to the Islamic State, whose cruelty tells the news received from their crimes against humanity.

What about the little known, and not less bloodthirsty, of the abandoned Central African Republic, with its crimes against religious organizations, do not leave Iraq or Afghanistan out of this context.

Finally, it seems that there in Libya, which already has its great difficulties, after the overthrow and death of Muammar Gaddafi, the oldest Arab and African leader, after eight months of revolts inspired by the Arab Spring, supported for a NATO intervention, after the capture of the capital Tripoli by the National Transitional Council, who ruled for almost 42 years his country in a dictatorial way.

Converge on its coasts, between Zuwara and Misrata, where people traffickers, collectives survival, sole objective whose knots of complicity are in cities such as Agadez, Niger, Tamanrasset Algeria or Khartoum, Sudan, where they capture those who have money and expectations for the trip to another world in search of what they lack in their country of origin and lock them up In miserable places of concentration, and then to embark them in battered and insecure boats, overloaded, at exorbitant prices.

Destiny, Italy, by that mortal road, where they have left their life, full of misery and needs, any number of human beings who will not have any of them pity, and have gone to the depths of that sea, or dragged later By the waves to the shores of a land that they wished to reach, but not that way, or dead in the holds or bilges of the insecure ships, measures that, to avoid that trade settled in the coasts of Libya, base of operations of these mafias will have devised the authorities, attempt to close the route, insubstantial procedure since they will be used to do so from other places already considered as an alternative to Syrian refugees, in the equation of conflict.

These contingencies, it is assumed, It is not in vain in this unlawful and inhuman activity that the exploiters of this route will take their years, which will have given them significant dividends, at the cost of so many lives that will have reached their goal or death, many others, many more than the previous ones, possibly.

Mechanisms that have been taken, in terms of establishing certain physical difficulties, will be in the morning part of the history of those frightening situations to reach the destinies, which will not be other than freedom, of which television and social networks have led to the table of the home farthest from the place of the events what there, even in real time, has been happening, contingencies derived from the construction of a fence to prevent access to those who try to use this city to jump to Europe.

Every time a route is closed, or its transit is made difficult, another, perhaps more dangerous than the previous one, opens the expectations of the desperate ones to evade the place of the events where the origin of its trip has been set in search of other horizons. There will always be Survival, sole objective another way to emigrate.

The tragedy of thousands of people who put their lives in danger to cross the Mediterranean Sea on board weak boats, for spaniards boats, boats with limited technical conditions or excess of people on board; has led to the fact that what was initially described as a migratory crisis, to which has been added that the humanitarian component has aggravated the situation.

Shipwrecks, as well as the successes achieved by those who were able to overcome the dangers of the sea, even with the precarious means of transfer, took place in a context of developing conflicts in their countries of origin which, due to their location and relative ease of access to the Mediterranean Sea, North Africa and the Middle East, they would be: Syria, Tunisia and Libya, Somalia and Eritrea; Increased statistics. The refusal of several EU governments to finance Operation

Mare Nostrum, a humanitarian and rescue program organized by the Italian Government, replaced in November 2014 by Syrian refugees, in the equation of conflict.

The Triton Operation of the European Borders Agency on 23 April 2015, the European Union's decision not to extend Triton's operational area to the area previously covered by Mare Nostrum; European Governments to triple the funds for border patrol operations in the Mediterranean in order to match the previous capabilities of Operation Mare Nostrum, a decision criticized by Amnesty International. The European Union later decided to launch a new military operation based in Rome called Eunafor Med under the command of an Italian admiral.

Mare Nostrum, which is relieved of its functions by the two subsequent operations, is supposed to be a program subject to a constant evaluation of the results, which will be reflected in both the disembarking, detention and return to their places of origin, such as painful death rates, and at best
Survival, sole objective.
Survivors arising from maritime and air operations) initiated by the Government of Italy to address the increase in irregular influx of people to Europe, during the second half of 2015 reduced the number of migrants eager to reach the Italian coast, and ass consequence the related wrecks of boats against the island of Lampedusa, small Italian island of 20 square kilometers of surface, considered by the undocumented the door of entry to Europe, obviously there they deprive the short distances, relatively, but not for that reason less dangerous, as it is 205 kilometers south of Sicily and 113 kilometers from the African coast, which allows in a few days, three or four days of navigation, according to the prevailing weather

conditions, who illegally pose those who achieve it will arrive in Europe, and those who, not by reason of circumstances, will attain it In and remain in the depths of the sea, or on the shores that receive them dragged by the waves, dead,

Chapter V. After the signing of the European Union Agreement, Turkey, new routes.

In view of the blocking of the Balkan route contemplated in the aforementioned agreement, resulting in the return to Turkey of all migrants arriving in the Greek islands, the search for new routes opens up the need to evade the prohibitions that are derived from the agreement, traffickers of people who deal with it by opening new roads, or reactivating some already existing and abandoned to other circumstances, routes that arise as alternatives and for the benefit of a lucrative business. Eight have opened to the trafficking of aborted human beings from their countries of origin, in search of other host countries.

Groups of migrants who arrive directly from the Turkish coast of Italy, skirting the Greek islands in boats, after embarking on the Turkish port, travel about 1,500 kilometers on a journey that lasts for days, number of people that exceed the capacity of these insecure ships, luck of some the arrival at firm coast, others found adrift, abandoned, on the high seas, to the south of Italy.

Some have looked for new alternative routes to the Balkans to reach Hungary, a route that could take them through Turkey, Bulgaria and Romania, all outside the Schengen area. Lampedusa, the Italian island, has witnessed the arrival of thousands of migrants to its coasts to which it has welcomed, many others have lost their lives trying to reach it, remains an option for those fleeing Syria, tragedies that have occurred on fragile barges, some coming from the Libyan port of

Misurata, others from Africa following the signing of the EU-Turkey Agreement, new routes.

Sub-Saharan Africa, including Pakistan, Morocco and Bangladesh; for many his death in Libyans waters was the corollary of the adventure in search of freedom, the stop in Algeria is usually common for Syrian migrants who choose to enter Europe through Melilla, their trip usually from Turkey, there they arrive by plane to Algeria where they cross the border via Morocco, many of the Syrians who have entered through this route will remain for months working in that country to be able to afford the high price usually demanded by human traffickers on the border of Melilla, a route that was one of the least problematic, however the route has been complicated since Algeria has begun to demand Visas to the Syrians, route to Spain by which the majority of the people that arrive are of this nationality, flow by this route that has been reduced to a great extent, according to the statues of the Spanish organization with responsibility in the area and the theme.

Crossing in winter by the new polar route, a little more sophisticated than the original, Syria, Lebanon, Syrian refugees, in the equation of conflict Russia, Finland, begins in Lebanon, there takes off the plane that takes them to Moscow, for something like about $ 1,500, with a visa requirement from the Russian Embassy, once in Moscow, a train will leave them in St. Petersburg , near the Finnish border, an increase that will arise after the signing of the EU-Turkey Agreement, which has given rise to the search for other routes like this one that we are describing, perspective of the migrants taking the "northern route", also called "polar route.

Which was the usual one for the entry of citizens of Syria and Middle East, acceding to Finland and Norway through its border with Russia, flow of emigrants by this route that has been restricted by the authorities of these two countries, closing its borders, which is intended by the Nordic country, Finland in particular, with these measures prevent the "polar route" from becoming the main route for irregular immigration. Another new route is that of Italy, the gateway to Albania: Syria, Turkey, Greece, Albania, Italy, which attempts by the Italian authorities not to

following the signing of the EU-Turkey Agreement, new routes.

International migration to Western Europe, subject to the request for humanitarian protection in Albania, and so long as there is no other way out to other countries, borders of this they have not been open, add to that, with the borders of Croatia, Slovenia, Serbia, Hungary and Austria closed, the only alternative left for migrants is to reach Italy by boat across the Strait of Otranto on the Adriatic Sea, a dangerous and costly route, an attempt by the traffickers to use them to take them to other countries from the Albanian territory.

Other migrants continue their journey by train, which stops in St. Petersburg, to Murmansk, a city north of Russia, and despite the temperatures, which can reach -30º C in winter, this route has become a of the fastest, cheapest and safest for the Syrians, as well as to go to Finland, fly to Moscow from Lebanon and cross Russia by train until arriving at Murmansk, very Syrian refugees, in the equation of conflict near the border with Norway, once there, cross the border crossing of Storkog by bicycle, since it is forbidden to do so on foot, stop and accuse of traffic of people who carry emigrants in their vehicles, deportations that Russia has been practicing who arrive from Norway through this new Arctic route, controls that were stricter and with reform of the Aliens Act, closing the borders with Russia to Syrian, Iraqi and Afghan migrants, which has motivated a detour of the route and increase of illegal people to Finland, through Lapland.

A new route, but less common, is the one that would take to Cyprus, this one, despite being the shortest, is not very crowded, although the distance is minimal, they separate only 105 kilometers, the journey that can last several days, it's very dangerous.

Migrants attempting to enter Europe are only a small part of those who are now seeking shelter in Turkey, more than 1.8 million, Lebanon, almost 1.2 million, or Jordan more than 600,000, the first of the following the signing of the EU-Turkey Agreement, new routes. Turkey, has absorbed most of the population for years and even the German authorities acknowledge that the country is "at the limit of its capacity": almost two million in a country of 75 million inhabitants, while Europe as a whole has problems admit that it needs to give asylum to a tenth of that figure, among its more than 500 million inhabitants. That is the current situation, so the picture becomes increasingly complicated.

Germany final destination?

Germany, intended as the final destination of the crusade, is considered the best by those who aspire to settle permanently in Europe, and the best, one of them, as long as they are as far north as possible, since they are more industrialized and that in any of them it would be possible to give the best prospects for those coming from Syria to apply for asylum and stay in the country, while the application is being processed, although the established rules, specifically the Dublin Regulation, European Union, Council Regulation No 343/2003 of 18 February 2003 on the Syrian refugees, in the equation of conflict 94 which sets out the criteria and mechanisms for determining the Member State responsible for examining an application for asylum lodged in one of the Member States by a third country national, which establishes as a principle that the application will be examined by only one Member State , this would prevent asylum seekers from being sent from one country to another, or that the system is abused and a single person submits several asylum applications.

It is the legal instrument that examines the asylum applications and in which those who have adhered to it, must remain until the solution of their requests, and as long as it defines its situation no citizen of Syrian origin, in this case, which arrives in German territory, will be at no risk of being returned, an argument invoked by the German authorities with this decision is that of a humanitarian order, but also an administrative one, in order to give back to those people a long and heavy, of paperwork and papers that make

Following the signing of the EU-Turkey Agreement, new routes.

Embarrassing the process and, ultimately, returning them is difficult for Germany, which at the same time gives them the possibility of appealing such a decision. Its reasons will have those in the north set their expectations, to reach the desired destination, Germany, now not to rule out what economics is concerned, could be an element in an equation in which, in his view, that of those who are they venture in their attempts, since although there are unknown elements, those who ponder when making their decisions, if they had time for that which is not possible since they will take them on the fly, there will also be variables, or elements , which by unknown people weigh the result will always be favorable in relation to the circumstances that existed when they made such decision in their country of origin, therefore only to note that the decision is framed in economic reason, indisputable value to consider, would be to do abstraction of other reasons that attract them and only those who face those complicated circumstances that forced it, will be able to

Syrian refugees, in the equation of conflict have the solutions, or look for them with the risk that comes from it.

Emigration, which is very important given that it is one of the countries with the highest rate of aging in the world (out of a total population of 82 million and a life expectancy of 81 years, almost 21% of the population has more of 65 years and the percentage of the same in the average age is 66.1%) European economic leadership that is subject to lose of not having access to labor that occupy the jobs that cannot supply by the lack of its nationals with an age appropriate for that labor activity, which has motivated the parliamentarians to analyze the present and future situation to reform the Immigration Law in a way that facilitates the access and permanence of that population in transit, the need for skilled labor to solve this imminent situation.

Chapter VI. International regulations, sometimes a fiction.

Whole families, including children and the elderly, from the Middle East, Africa, the Western Balkans and South Asia, try to reach Europe, in search of the legal figure of Refugees, who, according to the subject that governs it, Convention on the Status of Refugees, adopted to deal with the consequences of the Second World War in Europe and the growing political tensions between East and West during the Cold War and in Geneva, Switzerland, on 28 July 1951 by the Plenipotentiary Conference on the Status of Refugees and Stateless Persons (United

Nations) convened by the General Assembly in its resolution 429 (V) of 14 September 1951.

Entry into force, on April 22, 1954, in accordance with article 43, Series Treaties of the United Nations, No. 2545, Vol. 189, p. 137; the benefit that would be applicable to a person who "because of well-founded fears of being persecuted for reasons of race, religion, nationality, membership of a particular social group or political opinion, is outside the country of his nationality and cannot or , because of such fears, does not wish to avail himself of the protection of his country, or who, lacking nationality and being, as a consequence of such events outside the country where he has his habitual residence, cannot or because of such fears he does not want return to it ", which is also happening in other continents, perhaps by other variables, but emigrants at last, host governments that will be responsible for their protection, once completed the formalities that categorize them as refugees.

The reality of today, which is far from being the same as the reasons and scenarios typical of the era in which the Geneva Convention was sanctioned, and what is International regulations, sometimes a fiction. Applicable to any international legal regulation in this case, such as partial reforms to national legal norms, Article 1 of the aforementioned Convention, in the amendment, according to the 1967 Protocol, whose geographical limitations and temporary limitations contained in the original Convention stipulating that, in principle, only Europeans who became refugees before 1 January 1951 could apply for asylum, provides the definition of refugee as: "A person who, because of a Fear of being persecuted for reasons of race, religion, nationality, membership of a particular social group or political opinion, is outside his or her country of birth and is unable, or because of such fear, is unwilling to use the protection of that country.

Or who, because he has no nationality and is outside the country of his former habitual residence as a result of such events, is incapable due to such fear, of being willing to return to it. " Essential element contained there is the " fear ", when the document Syrian refugees, in the equation of conflict Original gave him the connotation of fear as denominator, intense sensation provoked by the appreciation of a danger that afflicts them and closes their tranquility, which in the end is translated in terror as maximum expression, it is enough to see those faces transfigured by what around them It gives them no longer that sensation of an extreme reality, but before them the certainty that this fact will be an undesirable truth, dimension in correspondence with the duration of the threat; which is what derives from the situation surrounding that society that is not an active part of it, but a consequence of the factors that forced them to take the determination to move away from the scenario that led, inexorably, to the loss of life as Last consequence.

It is also known as a migratory crisis (Syria is the country that has generated the largest number of internally displaced 7.6 million refugees worldwide: 3.88 million at the end of 2014. Afghanistan: 2.59 million and Somalia: 1.1 million are the countries that generate more refugees in the Mediterranean) or International regulations, sometimes a fiction. Refugee Crisis in Europe is the critical humanitarian situation that has intensified in 2015 as a result of the increased uncontrolled flow of migrants, asylum-seekers, economic migrants and other vulnerable migrants, who together share irregular European Union countries.

And by transnational criminal networks of smuggling of migrants, which exposes them to transport in dangerous or degrading conditions and trafficking in persons, for the purpose of exploiting the most vulnerable, mainly women and children. UNHCR and the Convention relating to the Status of Refugees the United Nations, through its UNHCR body, considers that Refugee, on a shared basis, that it is possible to call all those who leave their countries for reasons Immigrants because they are migrating, and in the end many of them are also refugees, in the practice asylum is granted to people fleeing from the Syrian refugees, in the equation of conflict.

Persecution in their countries of origin, which has been one of the main efforts of countries that are not in the area of conflict, their limits have been approached by those who evade, protection of those who in principle called Refugees, principal mandate of UNHCR; Was created to deal with those who, during and after World War II, survived the Holocaust, who moved westward to territories liberated by the Allies and housed in camps and urban centers built for that purpose on the German side occupied by the Allies , As well as in Austria and Italy, for those who expected to leave Europe, mostly Jews in the occupied areas.

The prohibition of forced repatriation of refugees is known as "non-refoulement," and is one of the most important principles of International Refugee Law. This principle is specified in article 33 of the Convention relating to the Status of Refugees, which states that no state "may, by expulsion or refouler (refouler in International regulations, sometimes a fiction.), to put in any way a refugee at the borders of territories where his life or freedom is threatened because of his race, religion, nationality, membership of a particular social group, or his political opinions.

Articles 12 to 30 of the Refugee Convention specify the rights of individuals once they have been recognized as refugees under the terms of the Convention: "All refugees must be provided with identity papers and travel documents that allow them to leave the country. " Asia and Africa are the continents that stand out because of the volume of refugees, the number of countries affected and extreme poverty. Southeast Asia and the Western Arab countries are home to the largest contingent of refugees as a result of the Vietnam and Laotian conflicts, the Russian occupation of Afghanistan and the separation of Bangladesh from Pakistan.

Schengen is the name of a town in the Grand Duchy of Luxembourg which is located at the border Syrian refugees, in the equation of conflict with France, Germany and Belgium, and signed in 1985, the Agreement, which came into force in 1995, to abolish common borders between member countries and establish common controls at the external borders of those countries; In practice, the Schengen area operates in migratory terms as a single country, as the first border-crossing agreement between those countries, Luxembourg, Belgium and the Netherlands. From that date, the Schengen area is known as the zone formed by those countries which have progressively acceded to the agreement and is the appropriate way to refer to Europe without internal borders.

The Schengen Agreement is an arrangement whereby several countries in Europe removed controls at the internal borders between those countries and moved those controls to the external borders with third countries. The agreement signed in the city of Schengen, from what became its name in 1985 and in force since 1995, establishes a common space called the Schengen area, whereby it can circulate International regulations, sometimes a fiction. Freely to any person who has entered regularly by an external border, or resides in one of the countries that apply the Convention.

In total, the countries that make up the Schengen area are 26: Austria, Belgium, Denmark, Estonia, Finland, France, Germany, Greece, Hungary, Iceland, Italy, Latvia, Liechtenstein, Lithuania, Luxembourg, , Malta, Norway, the Netherlands, Poland, Portugal, the Czech Republic, Sweden and Switzerland. The latter country voted on 9 February 2014 in a referendum to restrict the access of European citizens to its territory, which may lead it to leave the Schengen area.

There are countries that belong to this agreement but which have exceptions in the application of certain points of the agreement and do not belong to the Schengen area, in that context the free movement of persons, as a concept emanating from the Schengen Agreement that meant the beginning of the abolition of border controls between participating States, as part of the institutional framework of the Union Syrian refugees, in the equation of conflict 108 European Union; has expanded to include most Member States and a number of countries outside the EU. The Schengen area should not be confused with the European Union, since there are Member States which are not part of the Schengen area and there are other countries which are part of the Schengen area and do not belong to the European Union.

Since the entry into force of the Treaty of Amsterdam, which took place on 1 May 1999, after being ratified by all the Member States of the European Union, it became the new legal regulation of the European Union, after having been The Maastricht treaty was revised, and its fundamental objective was to create an area of freedom, security and common justice, with particular emphasis on several key aspects, namely employment, free movement of citizens, justice, common foreign and security policy And institutional reform, in order to deal with the arrival of new members, issues that had remained pending at Maastricht and International regulations, sometimes a fiction.

Treaty, the free movement of persons in the territory of the European Union from its Member States was established in accordance with the Schengen Agreement, a legal instrument which was integrated into the institutional framework of the European Union in a protocol annexed to the Treaty of Amsterdam, and by virtue of this protocol the new Member States of the European Union, those who entered after 1999, must apply the entire Schengen agreement, when the Council of the European Union determines that the conditions for this are fulfilled, freedom of movement between countries in the Schengen area may be temporarily suspended in exceptional circumstances, which has already occurred on several occasions.

The entry into force of the Convention implementing the Agreement or the Schengen Agreement entails the abolition of checks at internal borders and the movement of such checks at the external borders, so that any person who has regularly entered the external border of one of the countries implementing the Convention Syrian refugees, in the equation of conflict shall in principle be entitled to move freely through the territory of all of them for a period not exceeding three months per semester.

The consequence of a Europe without frontiers, as an indispensable element for effective European unity, derives from this agreement, which deals mainly with the abolition of controls at the common borders between EU Member States, in order to achieve the free movement of goods and services, as well as the establishment of police and judicial cooperation measures, and harmonization of legislation on visas, narcotics, weapons and explosives, etc. Schengen is more than a treaty, since it establishes new terms with a more universal content.

Nationals of a country that has signed the Schengen Agreement, and travel to another that is also part of this treaty, do not need a passport or visa, the national identity document of each country will be sufficient to identify, although not necessary, however, the authorities recommend International regulations, sometimes a fiction.

Carry a passport to avoid problems in case of emergency or unexpected closure of borders in case of risk to the security of any country, on the other hand, citizens and their families can freely establish their residence in any of these countries, if a family member is not a national of a member state, he / she benefits from the same right as the citizen of which he / she is accompanied. Case, you may need to issue a short-stay residential visa.

Residency cards are equivalent to this type of visa. Although there are European Union countries that are not part of the Schengen area, such as the United Kingdom and Ireland, which is now under study with the Brexit, they have signed the Treaty allowing the free movement of European citizens. Travel from any country in the Schengen area to any other country in the European Union, or vice versa, can be done only with the national identity document or passport, however this does not apply to foreign citizens, resident or not Union Syrian refugees, in the equation of conflict European Union, who will need to fulfill the requirements requested by the different countries to enter them, being able to be different from the ones requested to the citizens of the Union. Foreigners resident in one of the Schengen countries who travel to another Schengen country need a valid passport and a residence permit in a Schengen country, holders of a residence permit issued by any of the aforementioned States may for a maximum period of three months.

Foreigners who visit one of the Schengen countries will need a valid passport and a visa called the Schengen visa, this document is the same for all member countries, so tourists save procedures when requesting access permission, so that the Visa is approved the tourist will need Schengen insurance to cover some basic expenses such as repatriation in case of emergency, legal assistance or medical assistance. It is important that the insurer has a branch in Europe for the insurance to be valid.

-Dublin Regulation.

The Dublin Regulation aims to avoid two situations: the " multiple refugee ", which consists of making several asylum applications simultaneously or successively in different Member States of the European Union in order to increase the likelihood of a decision positive; and " refugee in orbit ", when asylum seekers move from one Member State to another within the European Union, without any agreeing to examine their application.

The Dublin Regulation stipulates that a person who has submitted an application for asylum in a country of the European Union and illegally crosses the borders of another country must be returned to the former. In order to reconcile freedom and security, this free movement was accompanied by so-called " compensatory " measures, which was to improve cooperation and coordination between the police services and judicial authorities to protect the internal security of the Member States and, in particular, to combat crime.

This was the context in which the Schengen Information System (SIS) was created, which is a sophisticated database enabling the authorities responsible for the Schengen States to exchange data on certain categories of persons and goods. A Europe without borders, that is the key to the Schengen Agreement, which allows the free movement of citizens of the European Union, the agreement, which came into force in 1995, facilitates travelers their travels because they do not need a passport or a Special visa, tourists from 42 other non-European countries can also travel without a visa through the Schengen area.

The Schengen Agreement, signed in 1985 and in force since 1995, allows the free movement of persons, goods and services by the countries forming the European Union, others such as Bulgaria, Romania and Cyprus could not join because they did not meet the requirements of Security. Iceland, Liechtenstein. Norway and Switzerland, which are not members of the European Union, have reached an agreement International regulations, sometimes a fiction.

Be part of the Schengen area. In total, the countries that make up the Schengen area are 26: Austria, Belgium, Denmark, Estonia, Finland, France, Germany, Greece, Hungary, Iceland, Italy, Latvia, Liechtenstein, Lithuania, Luxembourg, Malta, Norway, Poland, Portugal, the Czech Republic, Sweden and Switzerland.

Refugees, more than a statistic.

From the application of legal instruments, arguing, sometimes and in certain countries, their status as Muslims, through preventive measures to avoid approaching them by their borders, manifest cruelty of some vigilantes to avoid it, and building fences crowned with barbed wire one of them, although others such as Bulgaria, Estonia, Poland, the Czech Republic and Slovakia, have also opposed receiving them, we do not know whether by applying this method or another one of its genius, or admitting them and if not by making its position more flexible.

Governments, after events that have sensitized the authorities, in the case of the child Aylan Kurdi, of scarce three Syrian refugees, in the equation of conflict his family from Kobani, north of Syria, a place under the rule of the Islamic State, a family group that also perished in the wreck, except his father; all this is a true reflection of the drama that this country is experiencing and obliges them, the situation, to seek asylum in any country, Turkey being the most welcoming, with

2,5 refugees and Syria occupying the first place as a supplier, not grateful to the to do it with 4.9 million people refugees and, if we speak of displaced people also makes its contributions to statistics with 6.6 million, occupying a second place, not very exalted either, such ostentation.

Making use of the information provided to us, and always from sources of whose reality little or nothing is doubtful, we have that in the region where the conflicts initiated in Tunisia with the Arab Spring, with the exception of Turkey, take place in the region. 4.5 million Syrian refugees, in only five countries: Turkey with 2.5 million, Lebanon 1.1, Jordan 635.254, Iraq 245.022 and Egypt 117.658, this in terms of information and referring to the end of the International regulations, sometimes a fiction.

Of the years that the conflict has, the one that fits the content, related to the scope of application of the Geneva Conventions of 1949 and its II Additional Protocols of 1977, more specifically with the Additional Protocol I, that develops And completes the common art 3 of the 4 Conventions "shall apply to all armed conflicts not covered by article 1 of Additional Protocol I ... relating to the protection of victims of international armed conflicts (Protocol I) to develop in the territory of a High Contracting Party between their armed forces and dissident armed forces or organized armed groups which, under the direction of a responsible commander, exercise control over such territory to enable them to carry out sustained and concerted military operations and to implement this Protocol; the results, according to the UN, about 250,000 people have died and 13.5 million need urgent humanitarian assistance inside Syria; more than 50% of the population is in a situation of displacement.

One in every two people Syrian refugees, in the equation of conflict crossed the Mediterranean in 2015, were Syrians who escaped the conflict in their country, If we talk about resettlement, in this case we write, since the beginning of the crisis in that country have offered 162,151 places in the world, which is equivalent to only 3, 6% of the total population of Syrian refugees in Lebanon , Jordan, Iraq, Egypt and Turkey, and at least 450,000 refugees in the five main host countries, 10%, need to be resettled, according to UNHCR, and the need for places to support a community that is Countries such as Qatar, the United Arab Emirates, Saudi Arabia, Kuwait and Bahrain, have not offered any seats and other countries, such as Russia, Japan, Singapore and South Korea, have also not shown any support. Which is so required.

While Germany has pledged 39,987 places for Syrian refugees through its humanitarian admission program and individual sponsorship, approximately 54% of the European Union total, the same Germany and Serbia International regulations, sometimes a fiction, have received 57 per cent of the number of Syrian asylum applications in Europe between April 2011 and July 2015, excluding Germany and Sweden, the remaining 26 EU countries have pledged some 30,903 resettlement places, equivalent to approximately 0.7% of the Syrian refugee In the main host countries.

Chapter VII. Final approach, after a long journey.

How many hundreds of thousands of families, millions of people in the world have been forced to move, perhaps for this reason, to be cornered, that is to say confined in the polygonal ones of their countries, to which little International community, little-known situations, scarcely in their places of origin for environmental reasons, for example, the climate displaced in Asia, that go unnoticed, silent tragedy of which they do not escape, and live mobilizing in their own countries, to which Is given the importance, which is not the case of the situation of migrants that is part of this work, which by the nature of the cases that arise in any Syrian refugees, in the equation of conflict part of the planet, due to its incidence, time and efforts to find a solution by international organizations and countries that are being affected by the number of people who are anxiously seeking a solution from governments to their situation; who are involved in the same: the governments of the countries of hypothetical reception and those that cause the problem, the emigrants.

What amount of population, of any gender, age or social or economic situation (who has economic power, and if any, are referred to as economic immigrants, which is another social species, not the common one) to leave by means other than the risks of the roads on foot, or by the seas, aborted of their countries, there Syria country where a civil war is developed that already averages six years, before the advance of the Islamic State, what has caused the flight of thousands of people from that country, human groups fleeing to Europe because of the conflict, and not for their own reasons but outside their will, migrations.

Forced victims who go through the conflicts that have resulted in a spiral of violence, escalation resulting in armed confrontations, persecution, poverty, massive violations of human rights; to face the difficulties of transhumance, then to find asylum in countries whose borders, which as such are violated, consider allowing them to rebuild their lives and that of the family, with which they have at least managed to leave their place of refuge, origin in view of the long-standing internal situation in that country which did not find stability due to the effects of the war and its devastating consequences.

Migration crisis overflowing in a Europe, which already with the opening of internal borders, foundations contained in the Schengen Agreement, and now with the EU-Turkey Agreement seems to be more than giving solutions to problems ha, or will increase, according to the most varied comments, by means of which the 26 European countries, Syrian refugees, in the equation of conflict there were 22 of the 28 Member States of the European Union, which were joined by the four EFTA countries to form an area, defined as the space that derived from the name of the agreement, where controls were abolished at internal borders.

That is to say between Member States, limiting such controls to the external borders of that area, and countries with external borders would be obliged to enforce border control rules; spiral that has convulsed before the wave of refugees who looking to evade the situations of their countries of origin; have complicated, even more, the scenarios of the old continent, with incidence in some countries more than in others.

The refugee crisis has focused on the Balkan countries, especially on the border with Hungary, which has become the gateway to the rest of Europe for migrants already on the continent, and in anticipation of the avalanche of those who want the border, Hungary completed the construction of a 175 kilometer long final approach, after a long journey half-way along its border with Serbia, which does not seem to have the desired effect of deterring the thousands of people seeking to enter the European Union through that country.

The authorities are continuing to build a second, stronger and four meter fence to prevent the number of people crossing the border from Afghanistan, Syria and

Pakistan from crossing the border , which is no other than let them cross that country, Hungary, to other richer European Union, all over Austria or Germany, at least towards Bulgaria, Estonia, Poland, the Czech Republic and Slovakia, who have expressed their opposition to emigrants, mainly because of their status as Muslims, destinations for other routes that have sought the redoubts of Greece, Italy, Spain and Malta.

Epicenter where their calamities originate, that of those who try to overflow illegally the borders, not forgetting that a good part of not being able to reach the possibilities of leaving the country opted for the Syrian refugees, in the equation of conflict, Internal displacement bearing in mind the consequences that derive from the metastasis of a war for all the confines of a country in an effervescence in arms, situation that has not changed, and this in relation to the time of elaboration of this work, more of a year in terms of days' gravitation, as it is observed that President Assad remains in power.

The territory locked in a confrontation between the various political and religious organizations, there the Islamic State, in essence successor to Al Qaeda, and Its eternal confrontations with Iraq, becoming part of the Syrian territory, including oil deposits and its infrastructure, its years in it carries, a decade rounds in term of years, where the geography belongs to each other, and against the President Syrian government, and participation of governments from other latitudes who with different interests enter the conflict in search of their own benefits, less the tranquility of that country in flames, since the Arab Spring.

And many years have gone by, and there dead, disappeared, displaced and refugees, taking as a reference the month of March of the current year, 2016, from whose source we make full use, UNHCR, in order to illustrate a little the situation in which the conflict in Syria is, and therefore the consequences that derive In those who are the most affected, the citizens of that nation in flames, people with few belongings have escaped from their lands, the displaced aborted from their habitual places of life, their homes, which are counted by millions, people or groups relatives, who go through those paths of despair looking for somewhere to get security, or protection.

And refugees in the face of the events in that country, a precipitate departure in search of what does not have their place of origin, Syria, neighboring countries that carry a wave that reach a significant number of 4,815,868 located in countries that with the UNHCR figures: 2.1 million are registered in Egypt, Iraq, Jordan and Lebanon; If it is in Turkey, according to the same source, 1.9 Syrian refugees, in the equation of conflict.

Capacity of reception of neighboring countries that is overwhelmed by those who in a violent way undertake long and dangerous journeys, death included in their thoughts, plus thousands of people who resort to traffickers that their lives in their hands traders leave, to make those uncertain days through the Mediterranean in an attempt to reach the longed for security that will provide Europe. Or the other routes, which is more dangerous and insecure.

These figures, already mentioned above, could be even higher since not all Syrians who have fled their country are registered in UNHCR's registers at the time of their arrival, a crisis which is the largest humanitarian emergency Is currently facing the organization, assisting them in providing refuge and assistance in this situation, that of the Syrian refugees, already accepted as such, which has become the greatest crisis humanitarian, which has lived in Europe and whose origin is not exactly in its geography, as it was, and this by painful reference during World War II, whose statistics give an account of the scenarios of war within the same continent; when an indeterminate, and no doubt doubting very high the number of people of any age and gender who try to leave behind the confines of their homeland plagued by the conflict in permanent development, more than 230,000 lives has taken the war and if the refugees took note of the information that serves as a livelihood, which has generated 11.5 million displaced people and an estimated 4 million have had to leave the country, including refugee camps located in the theater of war or under the domination of the organizations in conflict.

Amount of people overflowing the sea and land borders, also harassed by the authorities denying them the passage, once the circumstances of the crossing have expired, arriving at the shores of the Mediterranean, information that Syrian refugees, in the equation of conflict transmit international news, radio and television, and from there they can see, in the imagination, the longed for silhouettes of Europe, ignoring everything with what they find, to the rejection of the arrival that awaits them, before tackling the fragile boats whose timber may be the urn that serves as a burial in the unfathomable depths of the sea, or having been exposed by so many and intricate land routes, before they could be reduced to 4 or 5 battered roads called routes, now after the signature of the Agreement between the European Union and Turkey, eight more have been opened, or many more, clandestine perhaps unknown by the authorities, more if known by traffickers of victims who in essence are those who in search of life in freedom and peace, to this they risk as the only alternative to achieve it.

In essence, the European Union rejects them, all of the countries that make it up, some more not so much but reject it in the end, and their reasons are based on the difficulties that already in case their societies and the economy of those countries already overflowing the possibilities of giving them hospitality.

Turkey, absorbing the most has raised its voice, the Balkan countries, special reference Hungary, gateway to Europe does not admit more migrants, and especially in the disproportion in the number of admitted, to the detriment of others, only those two Examples, underlining in all the political element, the origin of the situation that originates in Syria, its enormous calamities, those of those who emigrate who carry them with them, not forgetting that a good part, when not being able to reach the possibilities of leaving the country, opted for the internal displacement taking into account the consequences that derive from the metastasis of a war for all the confines of a country in armed effervescence, situation that has not changed, and this in relation to the time of elaboration of this work, more of a Year in terms of the gravitation of days, when: Assad still remains in power.

The territory embodied in a confrontation between the various organizations, political and religious; the Islamic State successor of Al Qaeda and its eternal clashes with Iraq, becoming part of Syrian territory, including oil fields and infrastructure; his years in it take a decade rounded in terms years, that are disputed portion of the property of the Syrian geography to each other, and against the President in functions.

Chapter. VIII. Of walking and walking down the paths of despair.

From these powders come these sludges, we make use of that old phrase fixed in the collective memory of the peoples, whose origin is their versions, the holy Inquisition seems that something had to do with it, interpreting it for the purposes of this work, the that we are already in the final phase, that because of the mistakes made, and could be identified as those powders, more than dust the desert sands, when the Arab Spring of 2010, so called that series of popular uprisings against dictatorial regimes, or pseudo democratic of the region, being Tunis, the starting point, and then Egypt; who changed government in a relatively short time, in terms of time, to which would be added others Syrian refugees, in the equation of conflict.

Countries of the region that made some democratic concessions to avoid total regime change, which Syria and Libya did not do, with the results that are well known: the Libyan revolt against the dictator Gadhafi, which ended up being transformed into a major conflict. A scale that ended with the death of the dictator in October 2011 and with the inability of the new government to control the country.

The welcome as the last hope.

If it is from Syria, to its situation that is the subject of this work, we have given the necessary and possible documentary coverage, which has motivated us to use the old expression, nowadays attest to its existence, tried to condense in some pages the existence of that state and the events that have given rise to the situation that today is lived there, and outside the same the one of the displaced and refugees that occupy statistics not desirable by any society, which for the year had in the order of about 23 Millions of inhabitants, a population census that today would yield totally different figures, as well as those off walking and walking the paths of despair they stalk around the world, thousands of them concentrated in shelters, or leaving their nails on the fences that separate them from freedom, from

Europe, in search of a new homeland.

As an Arab republic, whose beginnings as a State account for the history of colonization in times past, the presence of European countries that settled in territories of Africa, and when the process of decolonization began after World War II, between In 1941 and 1946, the French abandoned their former colony, and since 1970 the dictatorship of the al-Assad family has been enthroned, which in its early days was led by the patriarch Hafez al-Assad, who ruled until his death.

In the year 2000, and assuming power his son Bashar, who despite the consequences of the civil war, begun in 2011, has remained in power. Syria, because of the fact that in that country has already extended to something more than 5 years, visions of civil war without possibilities of solving, is but one of Syrian refugees, in the equation of conflict.

The many areas of disaster after the Arab Spring years, from its beginnings, let us also see, although it has not been an issue to deal with in this long journey: the dismemberment of Iraq as a unitary state, under the triple burden of Sunni alienation, Shi'a and the Kurdish separation, and the terrorism of the Islamic State continue at an overwhelming rate, the consequences of which are observed daily through the international media; motivate to glimpse that this 2016, was the year whose results pointed to consider it like an unprecedented humanitarian crisis.

Already at the end of the routes traveled by the need to leave land in the middle, that separates them from the war that has forced them to make that decision, three in its origins (one more, open between Mauritania and Mali, of Visa by Algeria, since the year 2015, which has forced to look for another course of action and has been only to move, by any means to Subsaharian Africa, to cross the desert until reaching Melilla); let us return to the defendants, of walking and walking the paths of despair known and open by the merchants of human need to leave behind the scenario where a conflict that already qualifies as humanitarian.

It is not an easy task to draw up a balance of results, which international agencies and non-governmental organizations, whose responsibility, in important part, depend on for the attainment of the ends proposed, which are not other than to escape the reasons for them. Have thrown their country borders to meet another reality that is nested in the mind; and to do this it is necessary to collect the numbers that bring a painful reality: refugees, displaced, dead, disappeared, human beings vexed, mistreated by the authorities, if not for the human miseries that are lodged in the mind and the actions of the merchants of other people's pain, and this is not easy for us, nevertheless we arrive at the end of the stage of this dark journey, days of pain and some smiles in the end, when not tears of joy and emotion for Syrian refugees, in the equation of conflict the end achieved, as well as pain for those who could not achieve the object of their dreams, not being able, good quantity, to cross the goal of longed for hope.

To speak of more than four million Syrian refugees, or about 95 per cent of all those who have left their borders, is to relate a large part of the population found in only five countries: Turkey, Lebanon, Jordan, Iraq and Egypt, that is to say those who left the conflict of their country to go to others, close to that one, but with their political situations in effervescence, that is to say their stability there was not exactly where it was, to say, in the first of the Turkey received 1.9 million refugees from that country, some 10 per cent of the Syrian population; Lebanon, 1.2 million, an important number for a country that already with its everlasting conflicts, welcomes them, in relative terms, as having to settle the maintenance of a population that already having this qualification, of welcome, not to doubt if these Statistics are derived from the of walking and walking the paths of despair UNHCR reports (whose call for funding for refugees has only reached 40% of what is required or requested from the international community, with those in Lebanon most affected and those encamped in Jordan More than 80%, is at the extreme poverty threshold) of which we are worth, official version therefore, its responsibility is to watch over them; Jordan, 650,000 refugees, 10% of the population; Iraq, still overcoming the invasion of the United States and its allies, carries with it the burden of 3 million who are subject to another classification, that of internally displaced persons, it is understood, and this in the last 18 months of the year in reference, 2015 , and of them, this country receives only 249,463, of the Syrian population and, finally, Egypt, that accumulates 132,375 people that identify to them like refugees.

To this painful reality is added that about 220,000 people have died; 11 million displaced people (without the option of taking the paths of freedom and peace, for the most varied reasons Syrian refugees, in the equation of conflict 140 Could interpret, while remaining, waiting for some longed-out cessation of hostilities, there would bring them insecurity, hunger, and fatality of death) that require humanitarian assistance, even if found in their own country, of which more 50% are classified as displaced, with little hope of being considered as refugees, or to find resettlement places, since of the 104,410 that have been offered to countries that are likely to accept them, where there is a large total of 400,000 Syrian refugees in In the five main host countries, the percentage is proportionally low in relation to needs, a situation that could be solved in parts if Gulf countries, such as Qatar, Saudi Arabia, Saudi Arabia, Kuwait and Bahrain. Are joined by high income countries such as Russia, Japan, Singapore, and South Korea; To resettle refugees of this nationality, Syria.

Germany, whose promise of acceptance of 35,000 people, through its program of humanitarian admission and private sponsorship, which will be equivalent to of walking and walking the paths of despair 141 To 75% of the total proposed by the European Union, in its entirety. All this, and the more, incubated in a conflict that has already overturned the five years, struggles to remain in power by President Bashar al Assad, against the opposing forces, those who also seek to seize power, who have divided, including al Qaeda appendages of Islamist groups, whose violence and cruelty are feared even by the rebels of other factions, equation of the conflict in which also intervene Russia with its usual bombings and the coalition that lead the United States, in the face of the presence of the Islamic State that controls part of the Syrian territory where a large part of the oil fields are, a resource that has allowed them to use to negotiate and obtain the wealth they hold.

In summary, this serious, part of the problems and greater results, which is coming out of the Arab Spring, in March 2011, in Deraa, which would be even a harmless action of a group of Syrian refugees, in the equation of conflict young people who painted revolutionary graffiti on the walls of a school in the city, several of them were killed, others tortured and arrested by the authorities, which incited the population to take to the streets, protests that spiral at the level national government, demanded the resignation of President Bashar al Assad, a response that was not expected by the regime's military forces, which further encouraged the anger of the population, demonstrations that spread during July of that year, for   all   the   country.

When from 2011 it is considered that no less than 4 million Syrians have been displaced from their homes, resulting in a complex international policy issue, resolution of which has so far escaped any application, other than academic ones, to Conflict resolution; as an unavoidable and legal remedy, to the United Nations Convention on the Status of Refugees, other conventions or agreements that govern the matter, opening borders, high temps of fire, little applied if violated when signed, or of walking and walking the paths of despair.

 Accepted, fights for the interests of each party involved in the situation, be it war or conflict, in the end it is the same in terms of loss of life, displaced persons and / or refugees; to the date of the conclusion of this long road, and with him the lines in this work, beyond the numbers of dead, disappeared, prisoners, displaced and refugees, are no more than being, and it is said with infinite pain since they are Human beings, rather than mere statistics that change day by day.

The armed conflict in Syria has become increasingly bloody, government and pro-government militias have intensified their attacks in civilian areas and continue to use indiscriminate weapons, apart from the use of chemical weapons that although proliferated in 2013 , International pressure to implement the Chemical Weapons Convention, if they had not been continued, Use of cluster munitions, at least seven types of them, proscribed all by the Conventions, siege to populated areas such as: Homs, Aleppo, Moadamiya, Daraya, Western Ghouta and Eastern, as well as Syrian refugees, in the equation of conflict.

If the armed groups are: Free Syrian Army and the Islamic Front, opposed to the government, also use weapons and indiscriminate attacks with projectiles of any caliber, light and heavy artillery from their areas under control, killing civilians in neighborhoods controlled by Government, known civilian targets, there schools, hospitals, mosques and markets.

Chapter IX. Syria, a country in its bewilderment.

Apart from certain references, there is not much of a case and for the sake of the brevity of the farewell of this page, Aleppo, with more than 2 million inhabitants before the war and dominated by Sunnis, where some radical Islamist movements Has a smaller number of Christians among its inhabitants, its population involved in what has been defined as a civil war, where the most varied struggles for power are settled, that Syria, in its entirety as a country, is a Scenario where Turkey, Iran, Saudi Arabia, Russia and the United States move to gain positions of influence and power in the regional order. The Syrians put the dead, of any more Syrian faction at last, where the forces fight in a fight, Syrian refugees, in the equation of conflict 146 Also, for gas and oil, where Russia tries to spread its business; Qatar planning to build oil pipelines that reach the Mediterranean; Turkey, with a confiscated economy and a currency depreciated by 40% in a year, needs an affordable crude supply and wants to increase its turnover with Iran, a major producer; A Saudi Arabia that is losing the spaces and that takes part to become of what considers to be its quota.

There, within that maelstrom of the war, Aleppo is located, to the northwest of Syria, very close to the border with Turkey; for the south of this country, traditional and everlasting crossroads of historical roads as trade routes, the ancient Silk Road is part of its history; to its 100 kilometers of the Mediterranean, by the west, and of the Euphrates river to the east; trade winds who puts us in perspective of what is happening there, and which, although at the beginning of the war kept her in the margin of the conflict, more in 2012, in its beginnings, February accurately, the death of 10 demonstrators, by the government forces of Syria, a country in its bewilderment Al Assad, during a demonstration aimed at finding the long-awaited democracy, and for the month of July the rebels facing the government, the east of the city, were in the hands of the insurgents, sending the Army to however, the government controlled rebel offensive against West Aleppo in July 2015 was not very successful in the interests of those who were confronting the government, an offensive that has since ceased to exist.

Government forces, increased by the intervention of the Russian Air Force, from September 30 of the same year 2015, and from what it has derived, perhaps one more attempt to end the conflict, a cease fire between the Syrian government and the opposition rebels, a national agreement between the Syrian regime, the rebel factions, and the Russian forces, reaching Peace, achievements such as laying down arms for a specific term, a truce extended throughout the country, and not limited to a Syrian refugees, in the equation of conflict,

Determined area, as has happened with Aleppo; signed a three way compromise: a cease-fire, a package of measures defining how it will be fulfilled and a willingness to enter into peace talks for a political settlement in Syria, with the exclusion of some groups or terrorist organizations by the Council UN Security Council, including ISIS and Jabhat al-Nustra.

According to a somewhat fragile agreement, Russia, which supports Syria, and Turkey, which supports the rebels, agreed to act as guarantors of the agreement, and determined that any group breaking the ceasefire could face reprisals from both Countries, the United States has for the time being been excluded from the Agreement, pending the assumption of power by the new President of the USA, Donald Trump, while Russia would reduce its military operations in Syria, no less certain that it would continue to support the regime.

The development of events in that part of the country has increased, as well as in the number of people trying to escape the intensity of Syria, a country in its bewilderment bombardments and the violence of the clashes of the groups in conflict, the contributions it makes to us, and we use them as a valuable first-hand source, IOM, when, almost in its exposition, 21 December 2016, in its final, allow us to reproduce that a "total of 358,403 migrants and refugees have entered by sea in Europe, especially in Greece and Italy," with a balance of deaths in the Mediterranean, so far this year, of 4,913, according to the Missing Migrants Project of the same organization, which indicates that up to "December 21, 2016, the average daily deaths are almost 14 men, women and children" Which suggests that "there were probably many additional deaths in the Mediterranean Sea and elsewhere, especially between North Africa and Spain, where this year the collection of data has been circumstantial, so many allegedly Small boats have been lost undetected. "

Data that change daily and an example of this is that to the amount previously contributed by Syrian refugees, in the equation of conflict 150 IOM, it appears that this week of December, in its conclusive days, occurred two new shipwrecks in which many people lost their lives, hence the number would increase, if confirmed, in more than 5,000 men, women and children, and although the increase in migrants would not stem from these clashes in this part of the country, other factors have increased, such as those arriving in Italy by sea from Libya, whose intention is not to go to Europe, As has been argued, when those who arrive in Libya, in principle with the intention of settling there, seek to escape the sea, because what they found there were abuses and violence, appealing, therefore, to unscrupulous traffickers who forced them to board boats not suitable for that dangerous crossing, aggravated by the harsh weather conditions at sea for these months, a consequence that is reflected in more than 5,000 people died you give.

Epilogue, something difficult to synthesize.

Syria, a country in its bewilderment when 2016 comes to an end, and with it the last stage of our journey through the confines of that world, the one we leave behind, Syria and the routes traveled to reach Europe, or wherever you can, the country where the war that has caused more refugees, in proportion, after the Second World War, by saying that it is no small thing, in terms of the consequences of that world conflagration, in terms of refugees or displaced people, and this so local as with so many and painful results, dead, missing, destruction of schools, hospitals, physical plants in general, no less sense the damage and destruction of buildings protected by international regulations, Convention for the Protection of Cultural Property in the Event of Conflict Arrangement and Regulations for the Implementation of the 1954 Convention, with its two Protocols, the first, 1954, which defines cultural property and the second, 1999, which strengthens provisions of the Convention and its First Protocol, relating to the safeguarding and respect for the cultural heritage and the Syrian refugees, in the equation of conflict conduct during hostilities, under the supervision of UNESCO.

Product of the conflict that develops there, and seems not to end, to make an epilogue on the details summarized and taken to these pages that precede the end has not been easy as each day that passed between the barbarism that comes from nature of these events when we try to finish, we are forced to take the utmost to the growing escalation of the conflict in a certain area, the city of Aleppo, to give us an answer and share about why there have been so fierce clashes there and, from there the corollary of the cruel attacks, in both directions and opposing forces.

And at the end of our journey full of encounters and disagreements with realities that from the outside world of the conflict has only a single idea, except that the interest motivates to enter by that reality as a search for information and deriving from It some knowledge of the situations that accompany those who by necessity Syria, a country in its bewilderment of survival they undertake such intractable ones, as dangerous and infernal ways.

Let us draw conclusions that allow the readers to understand a little better what this crisis means, and to derive it in humanitarian terms, and from there to contribute to answering questions that are asked, or what we are doing: what to expect from that war when confrontation between the forces in conflict: the government, and the militias that support it, continue without ceasing and with any type of arms to refuse to the delivery of the power? Already putting behind the bars those who do not share their political conceptions; disappeared and tortured; Countless displaced persons and refugees; total absence of the most basic principle on which human rights rest, due process, one of them.

But it is that those who oppose the government of al-Assad, the Islamic State, or in other terms ISIS, and al-Qaeda with their agency in Syria, Jabhat al-Nusra, have not responded with equal, or worse, cruelty where rape, kidnapping, torture, summary executions, which spread throughout the world Syrian refugees, in the equation of conflict of social networks, modern techniques of technology and communications and information that make perverse use and diffusion in this globalized world?

And deliberate and indiscriminate attacks against civil groups, cult churches, schools, cultural assets protected by international norms, hospitals and what is even more inhuman, the incorporation of children into combat factions where they should be is in the Classrooms.

The spread and increase of the fighting have left a humanitarian crisis with millions of displaced and asylum seekers to neighboring governments, besides the migrants, who in search of the qualification of refugees have crossed the borders of the European countries carrying with it a Situation in the old continent of unthinkable dimensions, statistics not increased by those who have left their lives in the depths of the sea, or by any circumstance not achieved their desired objective.

To this date, January 6, 2017 and making full use of IOM's information, we transcribed the same ones by mentioning that more migrants died crossing the Mediterranean Sea towards Europe in 2016 than in previous years, "... at least 363,348 people crossed the sea, most towards Italy and Greece, but an additional 5079 died or disappeared along the way ... a call was made, from the direction of this organization that Europe's frustration with an endless cycle of migrant rescue followed by reports of shipwrecks and further drowning will continue until governments in the region find a way to handle migration in a holistic way ... find creative measures to allow safe and legal migration, which could be achieved through work visas, family reunification or protection status "; moreover, stresses this chronicler, that this would be to give solution to the problem in its origins, there: wars, famines, violation of human rights, corruption of dictatorial and democratic governments also, if there were, Syrian refugees, in the equation of conflict presence of national and international economic interests, biased applications of the religious principles practiced by the different factions in conflict, in particular: humanize the war a little more, if this would fit as an expression, possible in the understanding that as a notion there is this criterion but in the extent to which they apply rules embodied in international humanitarian regulations.

The impression that we have after this long journey in the footsteps of the Syrian emigrants is reflected in the face of the survivors who have managed to overcome the circumstances at the end of this strenuous journey. How many of them did not, and their bodies would have been wrapped in ice in those mountains of the Arctic, or in the depths of the Mediterranean Sea, whose coffins were nothing more than the lumbering of a fragile craft that served them as hope. Routes of pain, three or four in its beginnings, sum of many others, four more, in saying, tangentially derived from an Agreement, with defects and virtues as it is to suppose of any act Syria, a country in its bewilderment elaborated by the hand of man, would result in interests that would benefit both the signatory countries, letters printed in those papers and signed by the representatives of the States, contracting parties that integrate the European Union and Turkey.

While the Agreements are expected to provide the desired result, the conflict continues there, in Syria, in full effervescence, Baghdad, Damascus, Deraa, Fallujah, Mosul, Palmira, Aleppo, borders, extremist groups, forces Of the government facing them, the powers making their own, other neighboring countries also, for the benefit of their interests; producing more cruel and more displaced people, more and more refugees, whole families perhaps, who struggle to escape from the reality that terrifies them and develops to the full without possibility of any solution, more if the humanitarian crisis in Europe escalate, scenarios of that Country in which these secondary actors, the civilian population, are trapped in a struggle that they do not Syrian refugees, in the equation of conflict generated and of which they want, as it may, to escape in search of Peace.

Referenced Bibliography.

-Acnur. Convention relating to the Status of Refugees of 1951 and its 1967 Protocol. Schengen Agreement, 1985 and Convention implementing the Schengen.

- Additional Protocol to Prevent, Suppress and Punish Trafficking in Persons, Especially Women and Children, supplementing the United Nations Convention against Transnational Organized Crime, Annex II, 2004.

-Agreement, 1990.

- United Nations Charter, 1945. –

-European Social Charter, 1961. –

-Convention and Dublin Regulation.

-African Charter on Human and Peoples' Rights, 1981. Supplementary Convention on the Abolition of Slavery, the Slave Trade and Institutions and Practices Similar to Slavery, 1956.-

-Convention on the Prevention and Punishment of Crime of Genocide, 1948.

-Genève Convention relative to the Protection of Civilian Persons in Time of War, 1949.

-European Convention for the Protection of Human Rights and Fundamental Freedoms, 1950

-Convention on the Status of Refugees, 1951.

-Convention on the Statute of Stateless Persons, 1954 (entry into force on 6 June 1960.

-Convention on the laws and customs of land warfare with annex: Regulations on the laws and customs of land warfare.

- The Hague, October 18, 1907.

-Convention on Slavery, 1926.

-Convention on Certain Questions Relating to the Conflict of Laws of   160
Nationality, 1930

-Convention on forced or compulsory labor 1930.

-Convention on the Rights and Duties of States, 1933.

-Convention on the Privileges and Immunities of the United Nations, 1946.

-Vienna Convention on Consular Relations, 1963.

-International Convention on the Elimination of All Forms of Racial
Discrimination, 1965.

-American Convention on Human Rights, 1969

 -Vienna Convention on the Law of Treaties, 1969.

-Convention on the Elimination of All Forms of Discrimination against Women
1979. - Convention against Torture and other Cruel, Inhuman or Degrading
Treatment or Punishment, 1984.

 - Convention on the Rights of the Child, 1989.

- International Convention on the Protection of the Rights of all Migrant Workers
and members of their families, 1990.

-Convention on the Prohibition and Immediate Action for the Elimination of the
Worst Forms of Child Labor, 1999.

-International Convention for the Suppression of the Financing of Terrorism, 1999.

-United Nations Convention against Transnational Organized Crime, 2000.

 -Convention of the United Nations against Transnational Organized Crime, UN
Charter.

- American Convention on Human Rights of 1969, the 1984 Cartagena Declaration
on Refugees. –

-"Principles and Criteria for the Protection and Assistance of Central American
Refugees, Returnees and Displaced Persons in Latin America" (CIREFCA-1989).

- Geneva Conventions of 12 August 1949 and their Additional Protocols of 1977. ICRC. Geneva.

-Declaration of Brasilia on the Protection of Refugees and Stateless Persons in the American Continent. Brasilia, November 11, 2010.

-Mexico Declaration and Plan of Action to Strengthen International Protection of Refugees in Latin America "Mexico City, November 16, 2004.

-American Declaration of the Rights and Duties of Man, 1948.

-Universal Declaration of Human Rights. 1948.

-Dictionary of War, Conflicts and Peace. Humberto Silva Cubillàn. Edit. Melvin. Caracas. Venezuela. 2013

-International Migration Law.

-Declaration on the Elimination of Violence against Women, 1993.

-San José Declaration on Refugees and Displaced Persons, 1994.

-Cartagena Declaration on Refugees, adopted by the Colloquium on the International Protection of Refugees in Central America, Mexico, and Panama, held in Cartagena, Colombia from 19 to 22 November 1984.

-Eurozone.

-Universal History of the destruction of books. Fernando Baez. Edit. Melvin. Caracas. 2004.

-OIM Glossary. International Migration Law No. 7.-

- Migration Glossary, 2000.

- Additional Protocol against the Smuggling of Migrants by land, sea and air, supplementing the United Nations Convention against Transnational Organized Crime, Annex III, 2000.

-The Protocol Additional to the American Convention on Human Rights in the area of economic, social and cultural rights of 1988.

-Protocol of San Salvador.

- Additional Protocol No. 4 to the Convention for the Protection of Human Rights and Fundamental Freedoms, 1963.

- International Covenant on Civil and Political Rights, 1966.

 - International Covenant on Economic, Social and Cultural Rights, 1966.

 - Protocol on the Status of Refugees, 1967

 - Principles Governing Internal Displacement, 1998.